Anonymous

Songs of the Settlement

And Other Poems

Anonymous

Songs of the Settlement
And Other Poems

ISBN/EAN: 9783744713924

Printed in Europe, USA, Canada, Australia, Japan

Cover: Foto ©Thomas Meinert / pixelio.de

More available books at **www.hansebooks.com**

SONGS

OF

THE SETTLEMENT

And Other Poems

BY

THOMAS O'HAGAN

" Come read to me some poem,
  Some simple and heartfelt lay,
That shall soothe this restless feeling
And banish the thoughts of day."
                    —LONGFELLOW.

TORONTO
WILLIAM BRIGGS, WESLEY BUILDINGS
1899

TO THE PIONEERS

OF THE

COUNTY OF BRUCE, ONTARIO,

WHOSE STOUT HEARTS AND STURDY ARMS
HAVE TURNED A WILDERNESS
INTO SMILING GARDENS,

THIS VOLUME IS DEDICATED BY

THE AUTHOR.

PREFACE.

MANY of the lyrics in this little volume have their root in the memory of pioneer days. They are blossoms of the "Settlement," retaining, the Author would fain hope, something of the twilight dew which nurtured and enwrapped them. May their fragrance help to sweeten the garden of life!

T. O'HAGAN.

CONTENTS.

SONGS OF THE SETTLEMENT

AND OTHER POEMS.

AN IDYL OF THE FARM.

O THERE'S joy in every sphere of life from cottage unto throne,
But the sweetest smiles of nature beam upon the farm
  alone ;
And in memory I go back to the days of long ago,
When the teamster shouted "Haw, Buck!" "Gee!"
  "G'lang!" and "Whoa !"

I see out in the logging-field the heroes of our land,
With their strong and sturdy faces, each with handspike in
  his hand ;
With shoulders strong as Hercules, they feared no giant foe,
As the teamster shouted " Haw, Buck!" "Gee !" " G'lang !"
  and " Whoa ! "

The logging-bees are over, and the woodlands all are
    cleared,

The face that then was young and fair is silver'd o'er with
    beard ;

The handspike now holds not the place it did long years
    ago,

When the teamster shouted "Haw, Buck!" "Gee!"
    "G'lang!" and "Whoa!"

On meadow land and orchard field there rests a glory
    round,

Sweet as the memory of the dead that haunts some holy
    ground ;

And yet there's wanting to my heart some joy of long ago,

When the teamster shouted "Haw, Buck!" "Gee!"
    "G'lang!" and "Whoa!"

Demosthenes had silvery tongue, and Cicero knew Greek,

The Gracchi brothers loved old Rome and always helped
    the weak ;

But there's not a Grecian hero, nor Roman high or low,

Whose heart spake braver patriot words than "Gee!"
    "G'lang!" and "Whoa!"

They wore no coat of armor, the boys in twilight days—
They sang no classic music, but the old "Come all ye"
    lays ;
For armed with axe and handspike, each giant tree their
    foe,
They rallied to the battle-cry of "Gee !" "G'lang !" and
    "Whoa !"

And so they smote the forest down, and rolled the logs in
    heaps,
And brought our country to the front in mighty strides and
    leaps ;
And left upon the altar of each home wherein you go,
Some fragrance of the flowers that bloom through "Gee !"
    "G'lang !" and "Whoa !"

THE OLD PIONEER.

HAVE you ever met the old man
  Coming down the lane?
His form, tho' bent with toil and care,
  Is free from every pain:
They sometimes call him "Guv'ner,"
  And sometimes call him "Dad"—
The boys and girls whose merry ways
  Oft made the hearthstone glad.

He moved into the settlement
  'Way back in fifty-three,
Before a man had come there,
  Or cut a single tree—
The only neighbors that he had
  Were wolves and prowling bears,
That in his stock of calves and lambs
  Full willingly took shares.

But the lonely hours soon pass'd away
 While nature sang her hymn ;
The robin piped his cheery notes,
 And hopped from limb to limb ;
The shanty smiled in broad, full day,
 The clearance opened wide,
And the farm that once was but a field
 Now stretched from side to side.

And so the "settlement" grew up
 In loving toil and care,
Starr'd with bright deeds of kindness
 As generous as the air ;
For hearts and hands were then but one,
 As generous and as free
As the gift of morn's bright flood of light
 Or shade of maple tree.

And here is where the strength lies
 In this our happy land,
'Twas builded by the grace of toil,
 By strong and patriot hand ;

And if a foe should e'er beset,
  Or 'proach our altars near,
We'll charge with all the spirit
  Of the old pioneer.

Then God bless the old man
  Coming down the lane !
His form, tho' bent with toil and care,
  Is free from every pain ;
He looks across his acres
  With their glory and their gain,
While his heart hath dreams of heaven
  As he comes down the lane.

A DIRGE OF THE SETTLEMENT.

THE wind sweeps through the forest aisles,
  In requiem notes of grief and woe,
For the great strong heart of the pioneer
  Hushed in death, as an oak laid low:
    Chanting a dirge at every door—
    Dirge for the Oak the Storm-King tore:
      " Here at rest is our pioneer
        In his little log cabin beside the rill—
        The stream flows on, but his heart is still;
      Here at rest is our pioneer,
      Wake not his slumber with sorrow's tear ! "

Where shall we bury this good, great man
  Who toiled in the heart of the forest wild?
Out in the field that is writ with his name,
  Lay him down as a dream-tired child :

" Here shall we bury our pioneer
   In his little clay cabin beside the rill—
   The stream flowing on though his heart be still ;
Here shall we bury our pioneer,
Break not his rest with sorrow's tear ! "

What would ye build to his narrow fame
   That knew not glory, nor gift, nor gain ?
His life touched God in a simple way—
   This be his column on Judgment Day :
     "Till then shall slumber our pioneer
       In his little clay cabin beside the rill—
       The stream flowing on though his heart be still :
     Till then shall slumber our pioneer,
     Break not his rest with sorrow's tear ! "

THE OLD LOG-COTTAGE SCHOOL.

THE old log-cottage school-house, John,
  I think I see it yet,
Just but a step from two cross-roads
  Where you and I oft met ;
The same board fence encircles round ;
  The bell—well, we had none—
But how we guess'd the time, dear John,
  By looking at the sun.

What anxious boys we went to school
  To learn to read and write,
Fill'd with the loftiest notions then,
  And futures just as bright ;
How proud we sat upon the bench
  And plum'd each word at will,
And smiling round—why, John, I think
  We're in the old school still.
2

Just look ! right there the blackboard is ;
   The teacher's desk in front ;
On either side we stood in class
   And read and "trapp'd" quite blunt :
But then those were the good old days,
   Ere style had stalk'd abroad,
And neatly prudish pupils now
   Would term our way "a fraud."

And then the games we used to play
   Upon the old school green,
How very little like, dear John,
   The games that now are seen,
When with a group on either side
   We hailed the ball with "Over !"
That, bounding down the old grey roof,
   In some one's hands did hover.

Well, well, time's changed, and with it, John,
   We've cross'd the path of youth,
And manfully bearing each his part
   Let's crown our lives in truth,

That when the silvery locks of age
   With death droop round in duel,
Our happiest thoughts may find a theme
   In the old log-cottage school !

THE FRECKLED BOY AT SCHOOL.

I REMEMBER well a freckled boy
   Who used to go to school ;
He wore a suit of corduroy,
   And always broke the rule ;
And whenever there was fighting
   Upon the old school green,
The freckled boy was in it—
   Fact, monopolized the scene.

The teacher "licked" him every day,
   And sometimes twice and thrice,
And on special swell occasions
   He'd get an extra slice ;
But in spite of all this drubbing,
   And his penitential life,
The freckled boy would fight again—
   Just thirst for new-born strife.

I remember well the old seat
    He sat upon in school,
'Twas chipp'd and marr'd with pocket knives—
    Which was against the rule :
His freckled face shines out there yet
    In wickedness and glee,
As it did in boyhood's morning
    'Way back in seventy-three.

And then the game of marbles
    Upon the old school ground—
If there was cheating to be done,
    The freckled boy was round ;
And if amid the stake at play
    An alley rare was in it,
You could bet your dinner-basket
    That the freckled boy would win it.

The teacher called him Edward,
    But the boys all called him " Ed ";
He sleeps now in " God's acre "
    With the slab above his head,

Where the flowerets bud and blossom
  'Neath the sky's vast chastely dome,
Where the games of life are over
  And the freckled boy at home.

THE OLD BRINDLE COW.

OF all old memories that cluster round my heart,
   With their root in my boyhood days,
The quaintest is linked to the old brindle cow
   With sly and mysterious ways.
She'd linger round the lot near the old potato patch,
   A sentinel by night and by day,
Watching for the hour when all eyes were asleep,
   To start on her predatory way.

The old brush fence she would scorn in her course,
   With turnips and cabbage just beyond,
And corn that was blooming through the halo of the
      night—
   What a banquet so choice and so fond !
But when the stars of morn were paling in the sky
   The old brindle cow would take the cue,
And dressing up her line she'd retreat beyond the
      fence,
   For the old cow knew just what to do.

What breed did you say ?   Why the very best blood
    That could flow in a democratic cow ;
No herd-book could tell of the glory in her horns
    Or whence came her pedigree or how :
She was Jersey in her milk and Durham in her build,
    And Ayrshire when she happened in a row,
But when it came to storming the old " slash " fence
    She was simply the old brindle cow.

It seems but a day since I drove her to the gate
    To yield up her rich and creamy prize ;
For her theft at midnight hour she would yield a
        double dower,
    With peace of conscience lurking in her eyes.
But she's gone—disappear'd with the ripen'd years
        of time,
    Whose memories my heart enthrall e'en now ;
And I never hear a bell tinkling thro' the forest dell
    But I think of that old brindle cow.

THE DANCE AT McDOUGALL'S.

In a little log house near the rim of the forest
    With its windows of sunlight, its threshold of stone,
Lived Donald McDougall, the quaintest of Scotchmen,
    And Janet his wife, in their shanty, alone:
By day the birds sang them a chorus of welcome,
    At night they saw Scotland again in their dreams;
They toiled full of hope 'mid the sunshine of friendship,
    Their hearts leaping onward like troutlets in streams,
            In the little log home of McDougall's.

At evening the boys and the girls would all gather
    To dance and to court 'neath McDougall's rooftree;
They were wild as the tide that rushes up Solway
    When lashed by the tempests that sweep the North Sea:
There Malcolm and Flora and Angus and Katie
    With laughter-timed paces came tripping along,
And Pat, whose gay heart had been nursed in Old Erin,
    Would link each Scotch reel with a good Irish song,
            Down at the dance at McDougall's.

For the night was as day at McDougall's log shanty,
  The blaze on the hearth shed its halo around,
While the feet that tripp'd lightly the reel "Tullagorum,"
  Patter'd each measure with "ooch!" and with bound ;
No "Lancers" nor "Jerseys" were danced at McDougall's
  Nor the latest waltz-step found a place on the floor,
But reels and strathspeys and the liveliest of hornpipes
  Shook the room to its centre from fire-place to door,
            In the little log house of McDougall's.

Gone now is the light in McDougall's log shanty,
  The blaze on the hearth long has sank into gloom,
And Donald and Janet who dreamed of "Auld Scotia"
  Are dreaming of Heaven in the dust of the tomb.
While the boys and the girls—the "balachs" and "calahs"—
  Who toiled during day and danced through the night,
Live again in bright dreams of Memory's morning
  When their hearts beat to music of life, love and light,
            Down at the dance at McDougall's.

A LULLABY OF THE SETTLEMENT.

FLOWER of the forest, nursling of dawn,
　　Sweet be thy slumber in cradle of light,
Rock'd by the song of the robin on tree-top,
　　Hush'd by the lullaby voice of the night ;
Nature, thy mother, is kneeling beside thee,
　　Filling thy dreams with the gift of her charm :
Sleep in thy downy nest, sweet be thy cradle-rest, sleep.

Flower of the "settlement," blossom of twilight,
　　Cradl'd and croon'd on the breast of the farm,
Pillow'd by Love, whose strong arms enwind thee,
　　Curtain'd by Faith that shields thee from harm ;
Sentinel stars keep their watch o'er thy slumber,
　　Sunbeams of joy fill thy chalice of morn :
Sleep in thy downy nest, sweet be thy cradle-rest, sleep.

THE SONG MY MOTHER SINGS.

O SWEET unto my heart is the song my mother sings
As eventide is brooding on its dark and noiseless
    wings ;
Every note is charged with memory—every memory
    bright with rays
Of the golden hours of promise in the lap of child-
    hood's days ;
The orchard blooms anew and each blossom scents
    the way,
And I feel again the breath of eve among the new-
    mown hay ;
While through the halls of memory in happy notes
    there rings
All the life-joy of the past in the song my mother sings.

I have listened to the dreamy notes of Chopin and of
    Liszt,
As they dripp'd and droop'd about my heart and
    filled my eyes with mist ;

I have wept strong tears of pathos 'neath the spell of
    Verdi's power,

As I heard the tenor voice of grief from out the
    donjon tower ;

And Gounod's oratorios are full of notes sublime

That stir the heart with rapture thro' the sacred pulse
    of time ;

But all the music of the past and the wealth that
    memory brings

Seem as nothing when I listen to the song my mother
    sings.

It's a song of love and triumph, it's a song of toil and
    care ;

It is filled with chords of pathos and it's set in notes of
    prayer ;

It is bright with dreams and visions of the days that
    are to be,

And as strong in faith's devotion as the heart-beat of
    the sea ;

It is linked in mystic measure to sweet voices from
    above,

And is starr'd with ripest blessing thro' a mother's
    sacred love ;

O sweet and strong and tender are the memories that
    it brings,

As I list in joy and rapture to the song my mother
    sings !

THE DREAMER.

MEN call me dreamer—what care I ?
  The cradle of my heart is rocked ;
I dwell in realms beyond the earth ;
  The gold I mint is never locked.

Men call me dreamer—this forsooth
  Because I spurn each thing of dross,
And count the step that leads not up
  A useless toil, a round of loss.

Men call me dreamer—nay, that word
  Hath burned its way from age to age ;
Its light shone o'er Judea's hills
  And thrilled the heart of seer and sage.

Men call me dreamer—yet forget
  The dreamer lives a thousand years,
While those whose hearts and hands knead
      clay
  Live not beyond their dusty biers.

A SONG OF THE STARS.

Down thro' the blue-clad fields of heaven
Singeth each star from its glittering throne,
A song of love and triumph—alone :
A song that the angels choir'd in the morn
When Christ the Babe in Bethlehem was born.

How old, how young this song of the stars,
Voicing the ages at noontide and night ;
Bearing to man a message of light ;
Trumpet of heaven and cymbal of sea,
Voice that was heard over dark Galilee.

Hark to that message of peace from the stars
Ringing athwart the hut-covered plain !
Shepherds have paused to list to the strain.
Far in the East God's love lights the morn—
Beams from the glories that Bethlehem adorn.

AN INVITATION.

COME with me into the mystery of Nature's shadow
and sound,
Where the heart of the past and the dreams of to-day
make holy each rood of ground;
Where the spoils of the years that have fled are heap'd
on altars of pain,
And the tears that were shed on each pillow of grief
are turned to glory and gain.

Come with me into the mystery of Nature's infinite
plan,
With its flower and fruit in heaven above and its root
in the heart of man;
Where the latent powers of things that are take form
and shape divine,
And the water of life at the wedding feast is turned to
red, red wine.

3

Come with me into the mystery of infinite love and
    care,
Where the planets wheel thro' the grooves of time and
    the swallows fade in the air ;
Where the thoughts that we utter seek home and rest
In the bosom of God with the Infinite Blest.

RECONCILED.

I saw two nations clasping hands
   Whose hearts had been estranged for years ;
The sun of peace upon each brow
   Dispell'd the darksome mist of tears.
Behind were centuries robed in night ;
   Before, the glorious dawn of day ;
While every peak on Freedom's height
   Flashed back the light of heavenly ray.

O sister isle !   O nation great !
   This day a victory hath been won
Far greater than the fame that speaks
   Through trumpet's tongue or lip of gun ;
This day Peace weaves a garland bright
   And heals the bitter wound of time,
Turning the sword with cruel edge
   Into a harp of golden prime.

CHRISTMAS MORN.

A LITTLE CHILD its portals oped
 When all was dark with sin and shame,
And Faith's eclipse found heavenly light
 Within life's ark when Christmas came.

The star that burned o'er centuries' brow,
 A radiant lamp of hope alone,
Now sheds its beams above the crib
 Wherein Christ chose His humble throne.

OUR OWN DEAR LAND.

OUR own dear land of Maple Leaf,
   So full of hope and splendor,
With skies that smile on rivers wide,
   And lend them charms so tender ;
From east to west in loud acclaim
   We'll sing your praise and story,
While with a faith and purpose true
   We'll guard your future glory,
      Our own dear land !

Your flag shall ever be our trust,
   Your temple our devotion,
By every lip your pæan be sung
   From ocean unto ocean ;
The star that lights your glorious path,
   We'll hail with rapture holy,
And every gift of heart and hand
   Be yours forever solely,
      Our own dear land !

A SONG OF CANADIAN RIVERS.

FLOW on, noble rivers !   Flow on, flow on,
  In your beauteous course to the sea !
Sweep on, noble rivers !   Sweep on, sweep on,
  Bright emblems of true liberty !
Roll noiselessly on a tide of bright song,
  Roll happily, grandly and free ;
Sweep over each plain in silv'ry-tongued strain,
  Sweep down to the deep-sounding sea !

Flow on, noble rivers !   Flow on, flow on,
  Flow swiftly and smoothly and free !
Chant loudly and grand the notes of our land—
  Fair Canada's true minstrelsy.
Roll joyously on, sweep proudly along,
  In mirthfulest accents of glee !
Flow on, noble rivers !   Flow on, flow on,
  Flow down to the deep-sounding sea !

Flow on, sweep on, sweep on, flow on,
 In a measureless, mystical key !
Each note that you wake on streamlet and lake
 Will blend with the song of the sea.
Through labyrinth-clad dell, in dreamy-like spell,
 Where slumbers each sentinel tree,
Flow on, noble rivers ! Flow on, flow on,
 Flow down to the deep-sounding sea !

MY NATIVE LAND.

My native land, how dear to me
   The sunshine of your glory !
How dear to me your deeds of fame,
   Embalm'd in verse and story !
From east to west, from north to south,
   In accents pure and tender,
Let's sing in lays of joyous praise
   Your happy homes of splendor.
      Dear native land !

Across the centuries of the past,
   With hearts of fond devotion,
We trace the white sails of your line
   Through crest'd wave of ocean ;
And every man of every race
   Whose heart has shaped your glory
Shall win from us a homage true
   In gift of song and story.
      My native land !

O let not petty strife e'er mar
  The bright dawn of your morning,
Nor bigot word of demagogue
  Create untimely warning !
Deep in our hearts let justice reign—
  A justice broad and holy—
That knows no creed nor race nor tongue,
  But our Dominion solely.
     Dear native land !

Dear native land, we are but one
  From ocean unto ocean ;
"The sun that tints the Maple Leaf"
  Smiles with a like devotion
On Stadacona's fortress height,
  On Grand-Pré's storied valley,
And that famed tide whose peaceful shore
  Was rock'd in battle sally.
     My native land !

Here will we plant each virtue rare,
  And watch it bud and flourish—
From sunny France and Scotia's hills
  Kind dews will feed and nourish ;

And Erin's heart of throbbing love,
  So warm, so true and tender,
Will cheer our hearths and cheer our homes
  With wealth of lyric splendor.
        Dear native land !

Dear native land, on this New Year
  We pray you ne'er may falter ;
That patriot sons may feed the flames
  That burn upon your altar.
May Heaven stoop down upon each home,
  And bless in love our people,
And ring thro' hearts, both rich and poor,
  Sweet peace from heav'nly steeple.
        My native land !

HEROES.

A POEM READ AT THE CANADIAN CLUB BANQUET IN HAMILTON, APRIL, 1894.

OUR land is dower'd with glory
From the east unto the west,
With rays of ripen'd splendor
That cluster on her breast ;
But the stars that beam out brightest,
And shall burn to the last,
Are the deeds that light our fathers' graves—
The heroes of the past.

O brothers, ye who gather round
This festive board to-night,
Whose hearts are timed to patriot words
That glow with love and light !
Recall with me the years gone by—
Full well ye know their life—
When patriots stood to guard our homes
In dark and deadly strife ;

When through our land a psalm of grief
    Smote every heart and door
With tidings from each battlefield
    Rock'd by dread cannons' roar ;
And mothers prayed and sisters wept
    With love and faith divine,
Beseeching God to guard our hosts
    Along the frontier line.

From Lundy's Lane and Queenston Heights
    The message speedily came
That filled each heart and home with joy
    And tired the wings of fame ;
At Chateauguay brave sons of France
    Drove back the stubborn foe,
With loyal heart and weapon strong,
    Just eighty years ago.

But not alone on battlefield
    Did heroes, staunch and brave,
Yield up their lives in honor's cause
    Our country's flag to save :

In savage forests deep and drear,
   Beset with hardships fell,
Our fathers toiled and sank to sleep
   Within each lonely dell.

Their memory lives upon our streams,
   Their deeds upon our plains ;
They need not shaft nor monument,
   Nor gold-emblazon'd panes ;
In virtues link'd through ages
   Shall their great strong lives flow on,
Inspiring souls to nobler deeds
   From patriot sire to son.

Theirs be the glory, ours the love,
   In this great cherish'd land,
Bearing the impress—-seal of heaven—
   And fashioned by His hand,
Whose victory is the ark of peace,
   Guarded by love—not fear—
Strong as the faith that consecrates
   Our heroes with a tear.

A nation's hope, a nation's life
　Be ours from east to west;
A nation's hope, a nation's life
　To fire each patriot breast,
That in the blossoming years to come
　Our proudest boast as men,
When bound by ties of nationhood,
　To hail this land—Canadian !

OUR DEATHLESS DEAD.

WHAT shall we sing of our heroes
   Who died on the field of fame,
Whose patriot deeds of devotion
   Our loving hearts proclaim ?
Shall we count the stars of their glory,
   And tell how they fought to save
The flag of our home and country
   Now floating above each grave ?

No ; ours is a simple duty,
   Devoid of trumpet or tongue,
With meaning far deeper and greater
   Than bard or poet has sung :
Our hearts must beat to their measure,
   Our feet keep pace to their tread,
If we would be worthy to honor
   The graves of our deathless dead.

The world is linked with cycles,
  Each lit with the glory of man,
Whose rays of ripen'd splendor
  Stream'd forth when freedom began ;
For Persian yielded to Grecian
  Till Roman valor won all,
Then the voice of the North rang loud and stron
  That Rome itself must fall.

Where now is the Spartan soldier
  Who fought with spear and shield,
Who lisp'd the names of the warlike gods
  That taught him never to yield ?
Where now are the Roman legions
  That answered to victory's call,
And smiled when the voice of Cæsar
  Sounded the march to Gaul ?

They live in the heart of history,
  But not in the hearts of men ;
Their names are red with the crimson stain
  Of Conquest's crime and sin ;

They had no message of freedom,
    They knelt at no altar but fame :
The gifts they brought to their vanquished foes
    Were slavery, sin and shame.

But the years have blossomed with new-born
        thought
    Adown long centuries' plain,
And the seed oft sown with Freedom's hand
    Has ripen'd for man—not gain ;
For the noblest thought in the world to-day
    Takes counsel with Freedom's plan
To snap in twain the bondsman's chain,
    And bid him stand forth—a Man !

Then honor and love and tears we bring
    To each grave of our patriot dead ;
To the soldier who hearken'd to duty's voice ;
    To the great strong heart that led.
We shower o'er each breast, long, long at rest,
    In rainblow blossom and hue,
The flowers of our heart, the flowers of our
        home—
    God bless the brave and the true !

4

TEARS OF THE MAPLE.

Sir John Thompson, Premier of Canada, Died at Windsor Castle,
England, December 12th, 1894.

I.

But yesterday its heart was joyed,
   It whispered love to brook and tree,
And felt in every root and limb
   The genial sun so strong and free.

Its pulse was timed to English oak ;
   Its heart was true to Northern Star ;
It grew in wealth of loyal care,
   Cheered by a gift of love afar.

It felt no gale that swept the land,
   For truth had girt its roots around,
And clasped it to a nation's heart
   Deep set within each rood of ground.

Now in its strength of power and love
   It feels the wound, it feels the cross—
The grief that bows our Mother Queen,
   The sorrow of a nation's loss.

From out that regal home where dwell
   The virtues that make England great,
There came a message dark in word
   That smote as with the edge of fate—

A message that a nation's hope
   Had fallen from life's throbbing sky;
That he who held a people's trust
   Fell softly in God's arms on high.

II.

O Maple, dowered with life and joy !
   O bleeding tree of bitter pain !
Our chiefest son, our pilot, guide,
   Falls dead upon the deck in main.

He loved the sunshine of your heart,
   A gift from England's queenly rose ;
He wrought two nations lasting good ;
   His soul so great loved even foes.

He built not on the shifting sands
  Of plaudits gained in dubious way;
He faced the right, achieved his plan,
  In clearest light, in fullest day.

The storms that passion rolled on high
  Found in his heart no anxious heed;
Within the compass of his love
  He knew no tongue, nor race, nor creed.

The magnet of his noble mind
  Found swiftly duty's firm decree;
He served his God in all his works,
  And loyal to Him was ever free.

His deeds are stars to light our path;
  His fame, a glory born of heaven;
His life, an arc of rounded toil
  To God and country freely given.

III.

O Maple, clad with Christmas cheer,
  How sad your dream of joy to-morrow!
When Hope had kindled bright her fire,
  'Tis quench'd by Death's dark plume of sorrow

And through our blinding tears is seen
   A ship that bears across the deep
The sacred clay of him we loved,
   For whom two nations mourn and weep.

O cruiser dark, with shadowy wings,
   Whose lips are tuned to battle's dirge !
Bear gently to our mournful shore
   Our honored dead through wind and surge.

May every star that crowns the night
   Drop beads of light upon his bier,
And angels weave a rosary bright,
   From Grief's dark pall and Sorrow's tear.

And O ye bells, whose requiem toll
   Speaks to the heart of life and death ;
Whose pulsing throb and deepest tone
   Are but a type of human breath !

Ring o'er his bier a chime of prayer
   Strong as a nation's grief and love,
That he who won a wreath below
   May win the greater crown above.

IV.

O Maple, robed in shades of night !
   I come from out your shadowy pall,
And leave behind the gift of pain,
   And break the bonds of Sorrow's thrall.

The greater life of him who died
   Is vital in our hearts to-day,
For deeds have power and soul to plan,
   To shape our lives, to mould our clay.

Whatever things are done for God
   Have root in soil beyond our years,
And bud and bloom in beauteous form,
   Devoid of earthly hope and fears.

This life is but the vestibule,
   The altar-stairs that lead to heaven,
Around whose feet the nations kneel
   And pray that peace and light be given.

And looking through the mists of years
   I see, as in a dream, a land,
Fashion'd and form'd in toil and prayer,
   A gift of God divinely planned,

Where 'neath the light of Northern Star,
With truth and honor for a wall,
A nation dwells secure in peace,
With God, our Father, guiding all.

JUNE IS COMING.

June is not here, and yet I feel
  'Tis softly tripping up the way;
The hours that throb thro' morn and noon,
  Have caught the glory of its ray.
I lean my ear to Nature's heart
  And count its pulse of anxious care,
That holds communion with a plan
  Deep set in dreams of toil and prayer.

June is not here, and yet my heart
  Drinks in the freshness of its morns—
The rose that blossoms on its cheek
  With light and love my day adorns.
The fields of heaven are tender blue,
  And clad with green are hill and plain;
While from each bud and blossom bright
  There bursts a sweet and glad refrain.

June is not here, and yet my soul
   Is touch'd with Nature's throb divine ;
The brook that slips thro' moss and mead
   Is to my heart a gift and sign.
O God, I thank Thee for this love
   That binds my soul in joy and tear,
That makes my life a hymn of praise
   To Thy great work, when June is here !

THE RAINBOW,

A Poem contributed to the Initial Number of the *Niagara Rainbow*, published at Loretto Academy, Niagara Falls, Ont.

Eternal seal of peace from God,
  With heavenly colors bright,
Spanning this earth with rays of love
  Wrought in divinest light ;
Arch of the hours, the days, the years,
  Since our new life began,
Symbol of Faith, and Hope, and Love—
  A threefold gift to man :

Above that altar crown'd with flood,
  In cloud of incense foam,
Thou build'st from the dewy air
  Thy many-colored dome ;
Glassing within thy subtle form
  The radiance of the sky,
Arching our lives, in tender faith,
  With love that cannot die.

A covenant of the peace that reigns
  Between two great strong lands,
Whose glorious heritage of worth
  Is gift of God—not hands ;
Where Truth and Honor have a home —
  An altar bright and fair—
Pure as the lily of the field,
  Wrapt in deep slumb'rous air.

O beauteous arch of faith and love !
  Shine through the mists of life,
And fill our dreams of toil and care
  With gift of prayer—not strife ;
Light with thy beams our darkest days,
  Rain down in mystic love
The joyance of the star-clad hours
  That fills each life above.

Link with a bond of sweetest joy,
  In memory fair as thine,
The hearts that plan, the souls that pray,
  Within Loretto's shrine,

That in the blossoming years afar .
    May shine out nobly good
The virtues of that Convent home
    Where dwells true Womanhood.

RIPENED FRUIT.

I KNOW not what my heart hath lost,
  I cannot strike the chords of old ;
The breath that charmed my morning life
  Hath chilled each leaf within the wold.

The swallows twitter in the sky,
  But bare the nest beneath the eaves ;
The fledglings of my care are gone,
  And left me but the rustling leaves.

And yet I know my life hath strength,
  And firmer hope and sweeter prayer,
For leaves that murmur on the ground
  Have now for me a double care.

I see in them the hope of spring,
  That erst did plan the autumn day ;
I see in them each gift of man
  Grow strong in years, then turn to clay.

Not all is lost—the fruit remains
    That ripen'd through the summer's ray ;
The nurslings of the nest are gone,
    Yet hear we still their warbling lay.

The glory of the summer sky
    May change to tints of autumn hue ;
But faith that sheds its amber light
    Will lend our heaven a tender blue.

O altar of eternal youth !
    O faith that beckons from afar !
Give to our lives a blossomed fruit ;
    Give to our morns an evening star.

NOVEMBER.

CHILL-CLAD, cold November,
   Autumn's drooping head,
Weeping skies, psalm-like sighs,
   Nature's cold, cold bed.

Dead leaves fall before me—
   Hopes of summer dreams ;
Naked boughs, broken vows,
   Mirror'd in bright streams.

Tatter'd robes of glory
   Trampled by the wind ;
Faded rays, faded days,
   Floating through the mind.

Days of gloom and sadness,
   Hours of sacred care ;
Lonely biers, bitter tears,
   Hearts in silent prayer.

TWO WORKERS.

THE man who plants a seed of corn
Aňd watches o'er it night and morn,
And prays the heaven for kindly cheer
To nurse its heart with dewy tear,
Is doing work of goodly part
Which gladdens hearth and home and mart,
And gives his name an honored place
Within the compass of his race.

But he who builds for future time
Strong walls of faith and love sublime,
Who domes with prayer his gift of toil,
Whom neither fate nor foe can foil,
Is doing work of godly part
Within the kingdom of the heart,
And wins him honor brighter far
Than ray of light from heavenly star !

IN LOWLY VALLEY.

Go forth, my heart, and seek some lowly valley,
    Beneath a sky of bright and tender hue,
From which kind stars rain down their mystic splendor
    And wake the earth with tears of heavenly dew;
Let not the summit peaks of distant glory
    Shut out the peace that reigns within the plain;
Better the flowers that bloom within the valley
    Than tempting heights lit up with arid gain.

Go forth, my heart, nor dream of each to-morrow
    That mocks the hopes and sunshine of to-day,
For life hath joys that grow within the present,
    But ripen not if touch'd by future ray.
In lowly valley, peace broods sweet and holy,
    Full of the vesper-tide of thought and prayer,
Bound by the golden clasp of love and duty—
    In lowly valley, life is void of care!

5

AN IRISH MOTHER.

HER dreams fill heaven and earth,
   Her love is a love divine—
Ripen'd through sorrow and time and tears,
   'Tis sacred as chalice of wine.

She kneels at an altar of hope
   When cloudlets have shrouded the day,
And her faith as a taper burns bright and clear
   Thro' the love that illumines each ray.

LIFE AND DEATH.

THE swallow skims through the air
   In fields of blinding blue,
While the heart of nature calls in joy
   To each billow of infinite hue.

Below, in a cottage, a mother sits,
   With the tears of grief her dower,
As she gazes into the cradle dark
   Where slumber'd her sweet, sweet flower.

O Swallow, that skims in the air !
   Do you share in each sorrow and woe ?
Do you hear the sob of a mother's heart
   Under the cold, cold snow ?

Joying athwart the dreamful heavens,
   Have you thought of the nest 'neath the eaves,
And the fledglings of care that left your side
   In the greening and glory of leaves ?

LOVE'S TRYSTING-PLACE.

Love met me at the hill-top
　　With glad and winsome smile,
And held my fickle heart enchain'd—
　　O just a little while !

Love met me in the orchard
　　'Neath a blossom-laden tree,
And storm'd my heart with longings—
　　I once again was free.

Love met me where the cypress
　　Is bow'd with Sorrow's tears ;
I kneel in homage at this shrine
　　Thro' all the rip'ning years.

TO E——.

LITTLE bird from sunny Spain,
 Fluttering in a tropic tree,
Sweet thy song and serenade
 O'er the bosom of life's sea.

Nature tuned thy heart so tender,
 Set its notes in chords divine;
Filled thy eyes with gift of wonder
 Deep as Memory's mystic wine.

WOMAN.

DIPPED in the instincts of heaven,
   Robed in the garments of earth,
Maiden and Mother and Queen,
   Wearing each crown at thy birth :

Threefold thy gift to the world,
   Pluck'd from God's ripening sky,
Tending the altar of life,
   Kindred to angels on high.

www.ingramcontent.com/pod-product-compliance
Lightning Source LLC
Chambersburg PA
CBHW021534270326
41930CB00008B/1250